Inanimate Apollyon

INANIMATE APOLLYON

BRAD LOWELL

authorHOUSE®

AuthorHouse™
1663 Liberty Drive
Bloomington, IN 47403
www.authorhouse.com
Phone: 1-800-839-8640

Published by AuthorHouse   11/08/2012

ISBN: 978-1-4772-9006-4 (sc)
ISBN: 978-1-4772-9005-7 (e)

Library of Congress Control Number: 2012921334

First Night Dreaming

A wisper
From deep within,
Taunting
The wraith from anchiet Caverns wispers,
Eccos' inside.
Face the beauty, splender.
all is yours...
All is promised to be forever...
Temtor, extrodinary bliss,
Then ends.
A reversol, chaos awaits...
with crushing teath.
An arrow marks the path
your descent, counch is ness
Never ending, lies inside,
a dream, bending the moment.
Swimming inside, Dragging inward.
Sworling outward.
sleeping but awake.
Till next you fall.
to be lifted
Chaos calm, Chaos sleep.

Temptor

Cristol clear, see threw
the flame, unspoken of pain.
Threw the eye of your desent,
A voice wispers.

To hold, the eye behold
Calming, wrenching, rwarning.
So far to go over.
To grasp, the eye, lies law, lingering
inward.
From the mouth of Chaos.
Turning inward then outward.

Spinning in brillant faction,
Bending controler, control,
"Master Them".

Chaos, wonder, madness.
Drifting further, Pain.
Revols ones own trooth
"Master them".

master I
Lonlieness Reclaim.
"Master them"
Master I
For what is lost
Inosence...

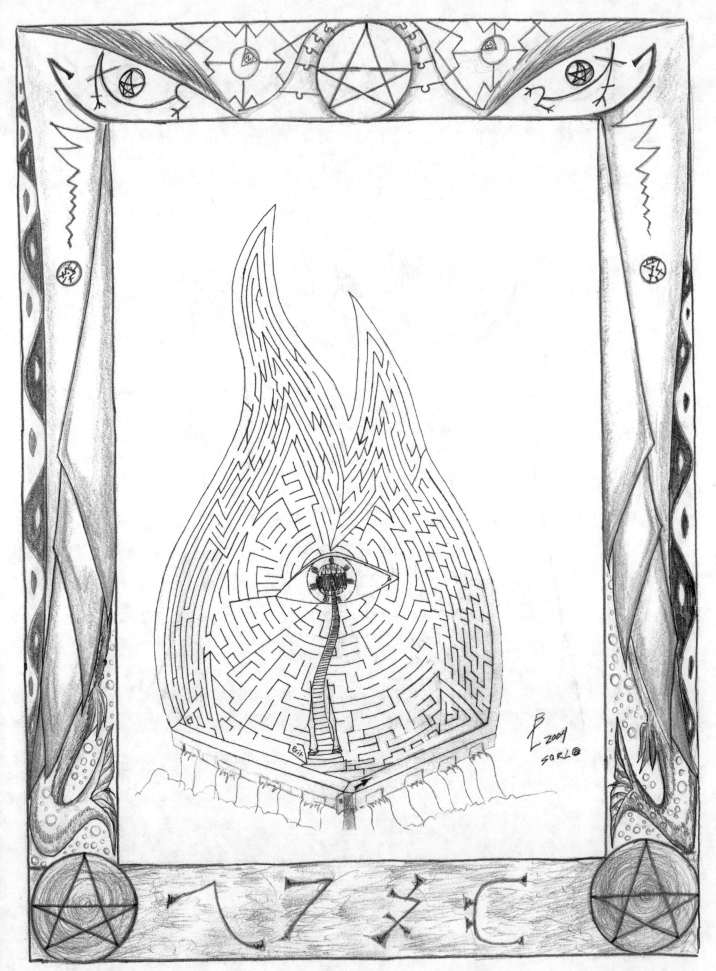

5

Wrath

Striking Lepard, magnificent
beast from a dark center to travel.
Threw these writhing walls swallowing.
some breathing.
A pasiphae, Intertwined in your control.
Travoling inward.
you face chaos.
With wraith we.

Twisted sprit of the fallen
Lonly beast sickened.
Nashing Fasten, From the
pool of ones ego.
Be your master
Grapes squeesed from feat.
beter than wine squeesed
from ones soul.
Caos Real.

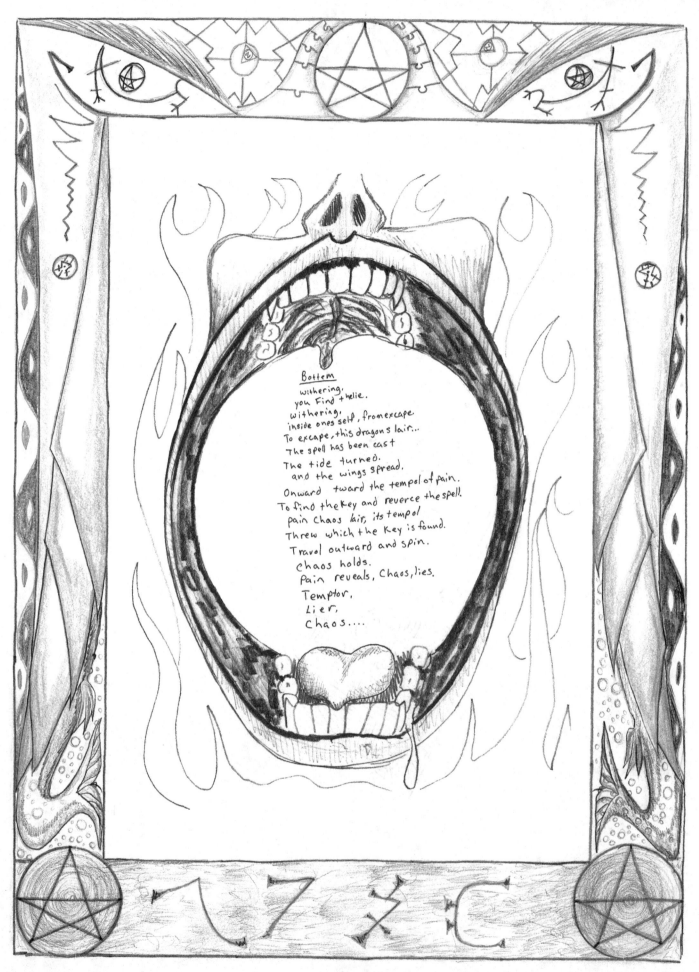

Bottem

withering,
you Find +helie.
withering,
inside ones self, fromexcape.
To excape, this dragons lair...
The spell has been cast
The tide turned.
and the wings spread.
Onward tward the tempol of pain.
To find theKey and reverce thespell.
pain Chaos lair, its tempol
Threw which the Key is found.
Travol outward and spin.
chaos holds.
pain reveals, Chaos, lies.
Temptor,
Lier,
Chaos....

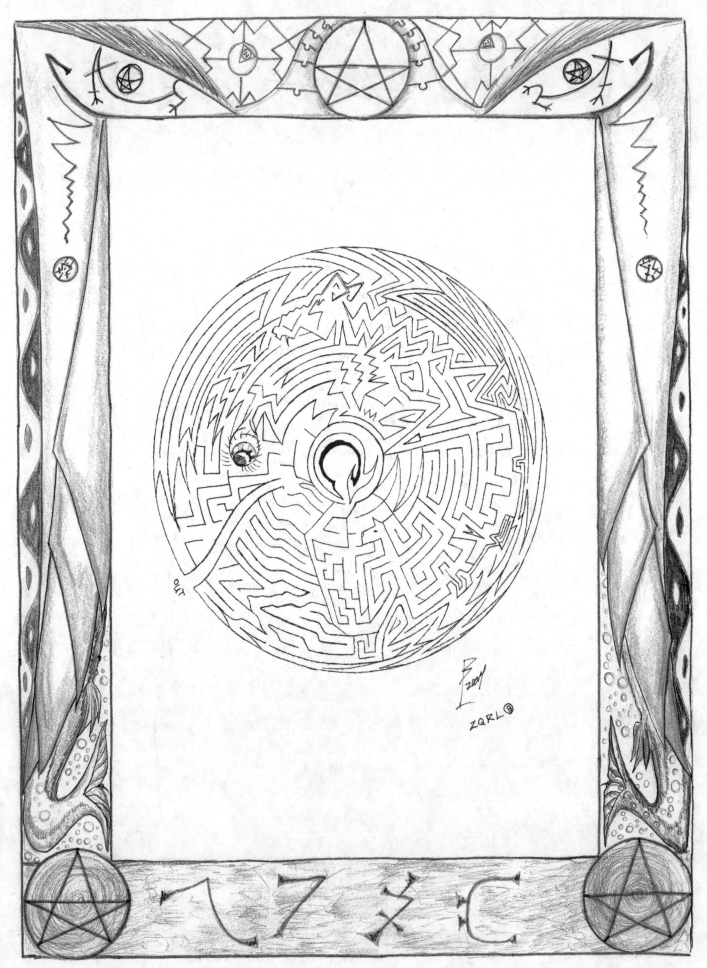

out

ZQRL©

Trooth

Intrude,
Intrude uppon ones self.
Inside the key lies from self.
Chaos inside, chaos outside.
from this now you hide.
Still swimming inside.
The key is found, in
the web in which you are
spun.
To late
The one faced is revelled
by nothing. Never wavering
is the key.
The key, pain confront
chaos looking inward.

To find the key which is pain
Insatiable...
Unrelenting...

The Key

So far,
Excaping ones self.
Torment of chaos, edging, Excaping,
further.
  Only faint the memory of
innerself, sacrificed,
true self.
  To the temtation of chaos.
New self waighing within.
Now shrouded in chains, cought.
  in pain, many fail,
falling back to chaos, forever
  Trapped in its tempol.
Covet the shroud, excape
what has been.
  The walls of the tempol
filled with misdead,
ones temtor to chaos
Temtor to self, to chaos lies.
  To self trooth,
becoming one again.
  The escape.

13

Reflection

Back to the flesh,
Returning from Chaos.
Whos teath once dull
have sharpened.
To have tricked the Temptor,
but never to forget, being
bludgeoned by Chaos in the
tempol of pain. The serpent
having been Revealed...
A foot forward past the
serpents lair. Back into
ones own tempol of flesh.
Now back may fate
be kind...
Allow one to pass threw.
Unlock trooth.
Pass threw the shadow of that
which sees all...
Past the glimmer past
the mouth of madness.
Yet you are not their.

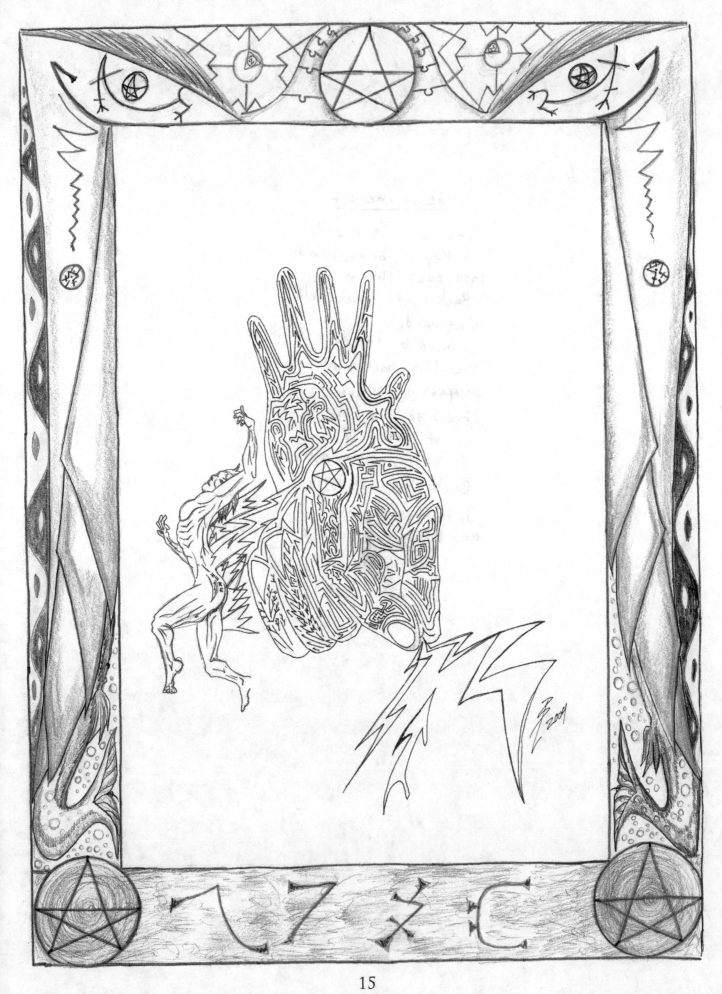

15

ode to the cat

The sin is revealed.
The Key is found, now to
pass back threw.
  Back into ones self,
is at hand.
  Tainted by the past
  Travoling back wards.
Surpassing curiosity
  Threw to the garden,
    of ones self.
    A bitter, narrow path.
  Back threw judging.
  Judging eyes into
and back from ones own subjection.

16

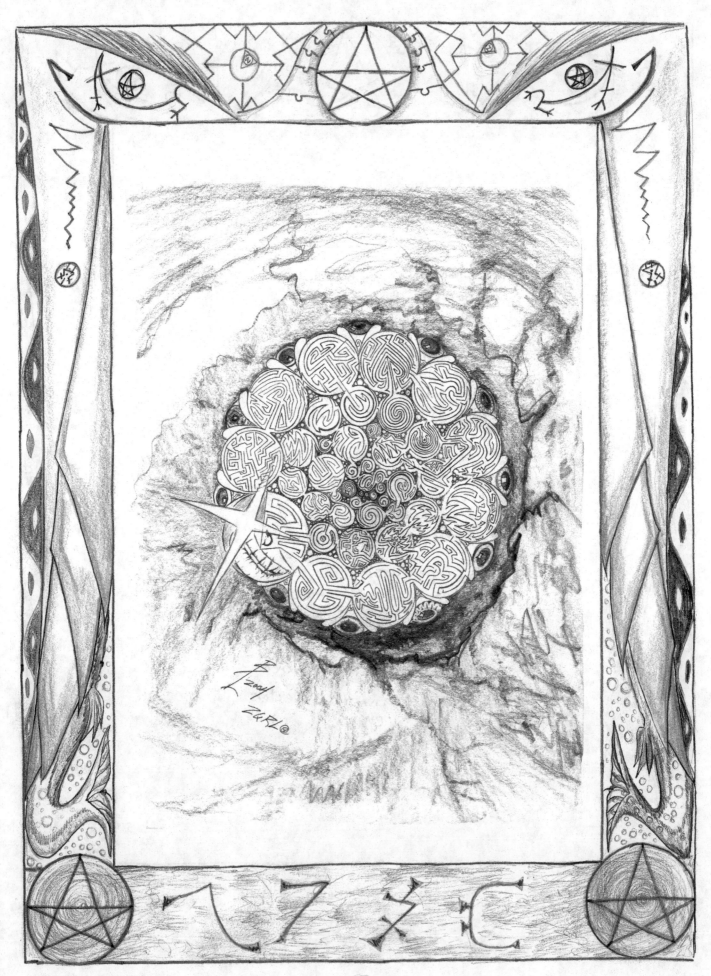

Poison to the Poisonier

Chaos in all you have........
backwards, or fourward, in ether..
Chaos plan has unfolded!
In ether pain is waighting.
Inner lingering;
Ever taunting,
A need,
Taunting....

In sleep is no refuge.
Awake to punishment and need.
To have seen the other side,
threw the eyes of the raven.
A thief,
Without perpuss.
To their then brake threw the
gate to your own emptyness inside.
Is were you waight.
Tho whom has swallowed
the seed, drank the nector
chaos....

18

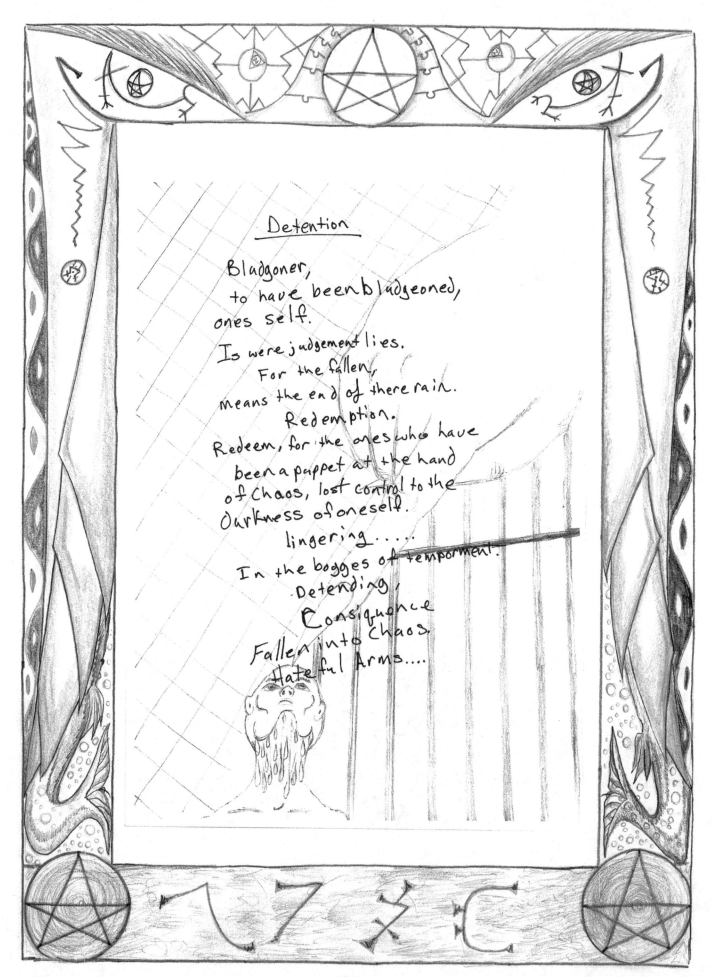

Detention

Bludgoner,
to have been bludgeoned,
ones self.

Is were judgement lies.
For the fallen,
means the end of there rain.
Redemption.
Redeem, for the ones who have
been a puppet at the hand
of Chaos, lost control to the
Darkness of oneself.
lingering....
In the bogges of tempormen!
Detending,
Consiquence
Fallen into Chaos.
Hateful Arms....

Judgement

And then I bring you,
or you bring me.
In torment wispers hard..
Is this injust?
Those wisperd words, told,
The mind...
"He stole,
Never Heal,
He wants them dead.."
All the ones' whom torment,
Each to each other,
Though ones self....
This one tied to the world!
You are one of the lucky ones!
Words from babes mouth.
once wisperd....
Chaos still ones temptor
Judgement wanes
A demon waites.....

22

23

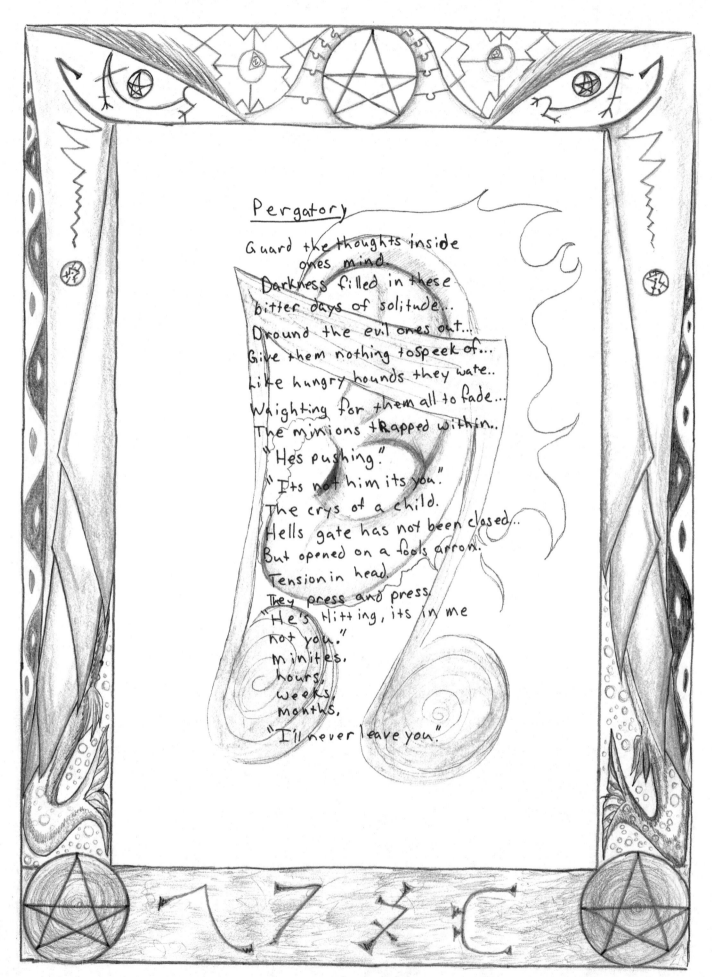

Pergatory

Guard the thoughts inside
    ones mind.
  Darkness filled in these
bitter days of solitude...
Drown the evil ones out...
Give them nothing to speek of...
Like hungry hounds they wate..
Waighting for them all to fade...
The minions trapped within..
  "Hes pushing."
  "Its not him its you."
The crys of a child.
Hells gate has not been closed...
But opened on a fools arron.
Tension in head.
They press and press.
  "He's Hitting, its in me
not you."
  minites,
  hours,
  weeks,
  months,
  "I'll never leave you"

24

Sealed

For pain and crys,
this tention brings...
Never to let them in again.
This thought accuring....
I did send....
Naked,
unhidden,
waighting,...
Sealed to pain,
Humbled and broken....
Chaos tryes to brake out threw me.
Humbled, I wate..
"Did you push?" yes...
"Did you lie?" yes...
"Did you lust?" yes...
"Hit and wrath?" yes...

Tormented is the tormentor,
in ones own sole,
Though tempted, in light
be healed...
Released from chaos grasp...

Ladder

So back you go,
Sinner.
And no you are not healed
from what you have been shown.
For ever Rember,
of snares and trappings.
lie there.
Having to face, the face of
ones self.
A tretourous path, wispers,
now only eccos of ones past.
still in ones mind.
So quiet the mind.
For the climb will be hard.
when faced with ones self,
Never fallen harder.

28

29

Fall

As if being suffocated
by ones own indignation.
The vines unwind,
The fear, still, Phantoms.
Anger,
Hate,
Paranoia.
Now knowing,
Food for the beast.
Tip Toe Through the mind.
Not so suductive to
ones self.
Still wispers, one hears.
Translucent,
World,
Now Numb......

33

Him

Angel!
Demond!
Hanging over ones head
Waighting..
For one who has no releace.
No control..
Sitting..
waiting..
In judgment.
Over this broken bird.
Feathers ruffled,
Head Limp
A twich
A wisper from ones mind,
he will pounce,
Ravage,
Brake,
Him....

Marked

A thought,
A trace,
A mark forever,
Trooth,
Closer running
Into light
The darkness senses the light.
But lingers like the sent of a wet dog.
The mark remains.
Never torn.
As ones self..
Formlessness...
Is thoughts in ones mind
Like face to mirror
Rule over deeds
wondering silent
day by day...

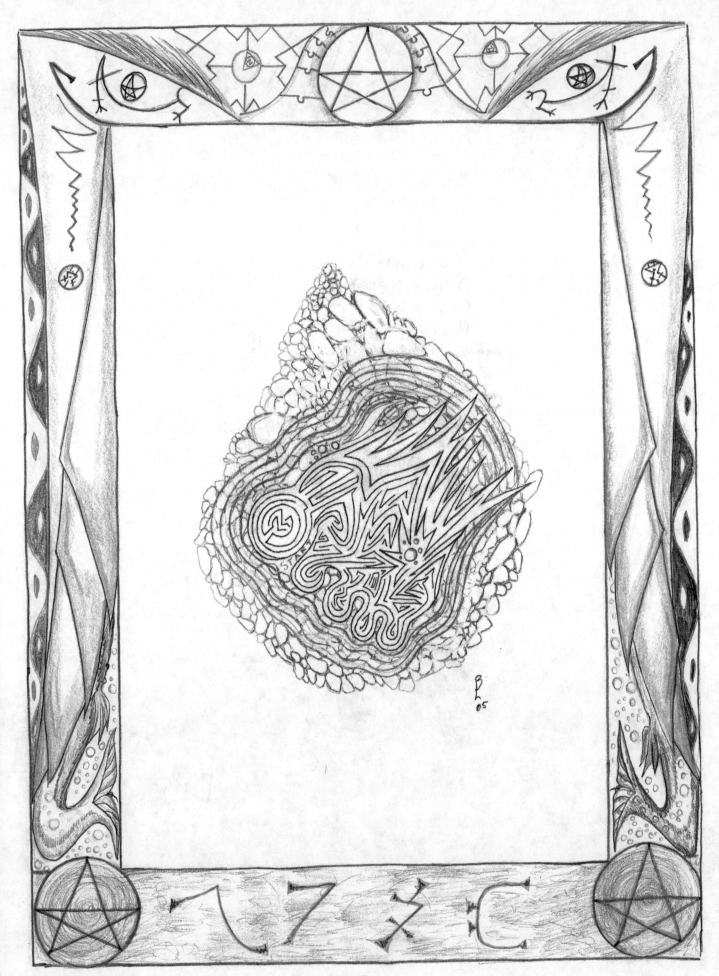

Hunger

Waiting,
yearn.
At one with hydra...
Do not speak,
Do not weep...
Harden
Make light inside the wall,
That from inside you,
now see out...
Though Chaos sits...
With his pusgalating mouth,
open...
Make no pretenct that,
The of ones self can,
Do no hate,
or harm.
Away Chaos,
No longer to feed on ones self....

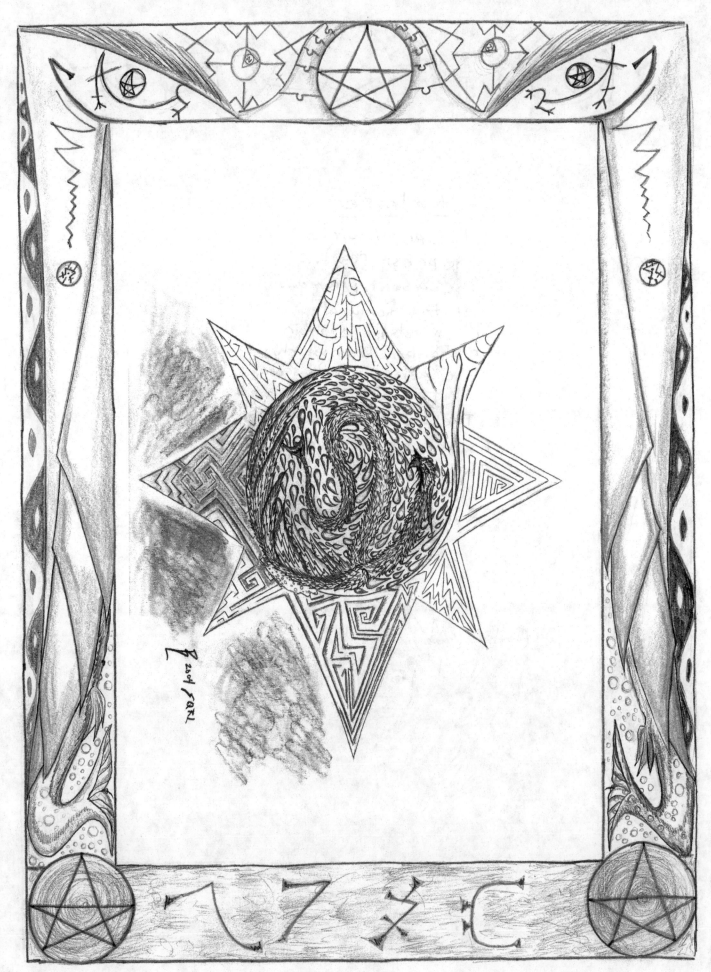

39

Release

The profit wrote,
The priest read...
The pesent prayed...
To the fortunate.
The masochist is within
a chamber from which,
The sadist, inflicts screams..

To war!
The masochists laughs,
As the satist tonts,
The innosent,
Screams,
Release......

Never Again

Ecohs of past Dream,
My mind erase,
Tortured past,
Travoling threw a nightmare.
When at it's end..
Never Look back...
Now what, is sayes
Never to speak,
Never to feel,
Never to send,
Give nothing to me
    Never Again...

43

From

A satellite
A microwave
A celestial presence
A ghost
A gray
A matter
A stone
A nother like me
A tree? maby
A fish or
A bee
Somewere under a tree
waighting for me.
Were or when,
might it be.
To never want, to see.

45

Something

In evening they fly.
In morning they feast.
On those that they
cought,
   To never release...
It happens in nature,
In all that we see.
   The preditor,
   The pray.
We can be either
   and never see...
So to the wise,
If whispers you hear
Take it with reverence
   and remember.
   The power to harm
   can be reflected...
   My Dear...

47

Some times

Sometimes it happens.
I'm thinking freely.
Some thing is nocking,
and Iv hidden the Key...
    But its tallons are reaching...
They are reaching for me.
I know that they are,
So silent I'll be....

    Gnashing...
    But only a wisper,
of the torment ones seen.
Is it still happening,
Someone elce besides me.
    I am no Island,
        so probably,
    maby...

48

START

To her

who ever she is...
Took pitty on me,
Faced slings and Arrows,
   on behalf of me.
while in this prison.
Gave my mind hope,
   when facing,
The creep...
Not fearing chaos,
Deflecting deceit...
From heaven they sent you
   To the pit
      Inside me ....

To myself

Never Forget,
This Journey of Chaos..
They lie and they tell you,
of powers for ones self,
To play in this,
Creates truble..
The other side,
screems,
Things of torture for some....
Unfortunet....
It tricks you with pleasure
but whe the gates close,
you'll see..
The chaos inside you,
It feeds on for free,
with things it will tempt you
To plant its seed...
Then it rides you,
Threw hell, and laughs as you bleed..
So be ware of the traps
hells given the intuder,
Can't see.

Printed in the United States
By Bookmasters

Printed in the United States
By Bookmasters